LETTERS FROM THE EMILY DICKINSON ROOM

To Peter –
one of my very
favorite poets & person.
Thank you for your ongoing
support of my work. I so
appreciate it & you.
Hope you enjoy
these poems
with love to
you & Dean –
Kelli

Letters from the
Emily Dickinson Room

Kelli Russell Agodon

Kelli Russell Agodon

WHITE PINE PRESS POETRY PRIZE, VOLUME 15

WHITE PINE PRESS / BUFFALO, NEW YORK

22 SEPT. 2010

WHITE PINE PRESS
P.O. BOX 236
BUFFALO, NEW YORK 14201

ACKNOWLEDGMENTS

Many thanks to the editors of the following publications where these poems first
appeared, sometimes in a slightly different form:

"Being Called Back": *Prairie Schooner*
"Believing Anagrams": *32 Poems*
"Coming Up Next: How Killer Blue Irises Spread": *Atlantic Monthly*
"Discovering the Tasmanian Devil is My Life Coach": *LA Review*
"Exam": *Southeast Review*
"From *The Handbook For Emergency Situations*": *Superstition Review*
"Ghosts": *Margie*
"Helping My Parents Shop for His & Her Coffins": *Prairie Schooner*
"How To Disappear": *Prairie Schooner*
"I Try To Plagiarize Moonlight": *North American Review*
"If I Ever Mistake You For a Poem": *Meridian*
"In the 70s, I Confused *Macramé* and *Macabre*": *Rhino* and *Letters to the World Anthology*
        (Red Hen Press)
"Journal Notes From a Consultation with a Dream Psychic": *Raven Chronicles*
"Letter to a Companion Star": *BigCity Lit*
"Letter to an Absentee Landlord": *Drunken Boat*
Acknowledgments continue on page 98.

Cover painting: "Her Garden," by Catrin Welz-Stein, used by permission of the artist.

First Edition.

ISBN: 978-1-935210-15-3

Printed and bound in the United States of America.

Library of Congress Control Number: 2010925982

For those who write letters to the world—

TABLE OF CONTENTS

Until you have a letter

How shall I pull through?

The fog is rising

*You don't know a woman
until you have a letter from her.*

—Ada Leverson

ANOTHER EMPTY WINDOW DIPPED IN MILK

"I've had nothing yet," Alice replied in an offended tone: "so I can't take more."
"You mean you can't take less," said the Hatter: "it's very easy to take more than nothing."
—From *Alice in Wonderland* by Lewis Carroll

I am the opposite of duende.
    I am the humdrum, monotonous, the blah blah blah

when you want dazzling, a passion
    flower with hipbones.

I'm not the voodoo that you do,
    but the bone from the salmon on the side

of your plate. My lips say hiatus, say corpse pose.
    All morning I make Ku Ding tea, serve crumb cake.

Trust me, it's not bitterness I carry
    in my blood, but the pulse and flow

of ordinary, the white picket fence
    I like to call my ribcage. Listen—

the faulty valve of my heart quotes Einstein,
    believes everything's a miracle instead of nothing is.

All around, birdsong and background
    music. All around, diamond birds and beetles.

To the mirror, I'm less than a gem. Some days
    I see green glass while others see emeralds.

I needle through this, trying to sew synchronicity
    into my stories. Sometimes I drop a stitch

and have to back-tack spiritus mundi to my hem,
    slide the universe beneath my slip.

I would live differently if I knew passion
    flowers would bloom in my bourbon,

if I believed randomness
    wasn't only a bone I choked on.

At night God speaks to me while I'm balanced
    in dead bug pose. He says I'm beautiful

balanced in dead bug pose, but
    I want to be the voice and not the insect,

the hipsway of tail feathers and not the egg
    broken beneath a wingspan of worry.

I tell myself I'm safe from extinction
    living in a marsh of marginal, a swamp

of so-so, but I'm afraid I'm becoming the common
    seagull. Deep down, hope perches in my ribcage

and its song is enough to make me soar.
    And this hum I thought was a murmur,

was another's words—*dwell, dwell*—in a voice,
    a ventricle, in the vital song of a hermit

thrush singing, *here I am right near you,*
    to the robin outside my window

repeating as I serve the crumb cake,
    the bitter tea: *cheer-up, cheer-up, cheer-up.*

BEING CALLED BACK

Nevertheless its steps can be heard. . .
—Pablo Neruda, "Nothing But Death"

In case of accident, call a priest,
     or so reads the back of
my Saint Christopher medallion.

And I want to engrave:
     Or 911. Or an ambulance,
but not just the priest.

I know the priest would come,
     offer everlasting life and pray
over my body, but I'm betting

on the medic, the EMT, the blonde girl
     who works weekends at the fire station
to keep her daughter in private school.

I put my faith in the hands of these saviors
     before I'll kiss the white collar
of the man who loves God the same way I love life.

I'm not ready to be called back. Not now.
     Maybe when my body begins to crumble
and needs every speck of energy to leave

a chair or revise a poem, then I will say:
     Just the priest please.
But for now, call anyone

you think could help, anyone
          who could pull me from the land of afterlife
where "eternal bliss" *sounds* lovely,

roaming the clouds with dead relatives
          or wandering a white fog
near the wings of a friend who died too young.

I imagine yards of cotton unrolling.
          God is remodeling the space
for the eighty-million new souls

who will visit this year, souls climbing
          the new spiral staircase.
It will be enchanting to encounter people

who've passed before me. I'll make a point
          to ask Neruda about death
dressed as a broom, as I keep believing I'll be swept up.

BELIEVING ANAGRAMS

—after being asked why I write so many poems about death and poetry

There's *real fun* in *funeral,*
and in *the pearly gates—the pages relate.*

You know, I fall *prey to*
                    poetry,

have *hated*
        death.

All my life,
        literature has been my *ritual tree—*

Shakespeare with his *hearse speak,*
Pablo Neruda, my *adorable pun.*

So when I write about *death and poetry,*
        it's *donated therapy*
        where I converse with
        Emily Dickinson, my *inky misled icon.*

And when my *dream songs* are *demon's rags,*
        I dust my *manuscript* in a *manic spurt*
        hoping the *reader* will *reread*

because I want the world
to *pray for poets* as we are only a *story of paper.*

COMING UP NEXT:
HOW KILLER BLUE IRISES SPREAD

—Misheard health report on NPR

It's the quiet ones, the flowers
the neighbors said
kept to themselves,

Iris gettagunandkillus, shoots

and rhizomes reaching
beneath the fence.
The shifty ones,

Mickey Blue Iris, the tubers

that pretend to be dormant
then spread late night into
the garden of evil and no good.

They know hell, their blue flames

fooling van Gogh, the knife
he stuck into soil before he sliced
the bulbs in three, nights

he spent painting in a mad heat.

They swell before the cut
and divide of autumn.
An entire field of tulips,

flattened. Daylilies found

like lean bodies across the path.
The wild blue iris claims
responsibility, weaves through

the gladioli, into the hothouse

where the corpse flower blooms
for a single day, its scent
of death calling to the flies.

DISCOVERING THE TASMANIAN DEVIL
IS MY LIFE COACH

He wants me to speak without language.
What can you say in a facial expression?
Can you find contentment in chaos? Disruption?

All my life I've been told
to speak slowly, use manners.
He'd like me to slurp a hunk of meat

from my dinner plate, break the wine glass
and guzzle the bottle. He says I'm improving
on my spontaneity, but there's room

to rip apart the wildflowers without feeling
guilty for what was. He says remember the time
your mother said, *Young ladies don't dress that way.*

He tells me to spin naked through a continent
being only distracted with rabbits disguised
as the opposite sex. *Try dressing as a tornado,*

find passion in every twirl.
He tells me he knows it's silly
to suggest I sleep on a full stomach

and destroy whatever gets in my path,
but he's asked me to be an innocent savage,
be the person the room stops for.

EXAM

Sometimes I still dream about their pink bodies
floating above my nightstand in jars of formaldehyde.

To calm our nerves the teacher told us these pigs
were never born, but salvaged from pregnant

sows after slaughter. I sliced carefully
with an Exacto-knife, opened the lids of its eyes.

Though I never spoke it, I wanted to
remove its organs and christen them

in the stainless steel sink. There was a girl
in my class who found her newborn sister
face down in the tub while her mom slept

drunk on the bathroom floor. I wondered
if death was the puddle of water beside her

and life was the spider that passed by.
The teacher asked us to find the pig's heart,

remove it and place it on the tray. I placed
my fingers inside its body and turned to the boy

next to me who was cutting off the legs of his pig,
one by one, and placing them in a line.

FRAGMENTS OF A DISSECTED WORD

Because it's easier to rename,
to change what I can't fix—
now *depression* belongs

to someone else. I mix up
the letters and say,

I'm just taking care of *Red's ponies,*
instead of having to say
I'm falling apart.

And I take this word further,
say I am filled with *sin or speed,*
piss or need, or deep sins—

deep deep sins.
But this word—*depression*
—I read it inside out: *persons die,*

a *ripened SOS.*
And when it's around, I become
a *side person,*   *posed, risen,*

I am *opened, sirs.*
I can rearrange the letters
but I cannot arrange it

from my life.
Like playing Clue:
it was *sis* in the *den* with a *rope,*

I keep waiting to find out
the ending,

Rose, I spend my nights awake
and all those years I didn't tell you,
I pressed on.

FROM *THE HANDBOOK*
FOR EMERGENCY SITUATIONS

When we were in love
I read you *How to Survive*
If You Fall Through the Ice.

You were determined not to
listen. You plugged your ears when I read,
Face the direction from which you came.

You told me love could be confused
with drowning. I said, *Use your elbows*
to lift yourself onto the edge of the hole.

You never wanted to live
that coldly. You moved close, drank
peppermint tea. I read, *Reach out*

onto the solid ice as far as possible.
You said our chances were slim,
we lived in a temperate climate.

What if you knew then
that later we'd find reasons to dislike
each other's sentences, how many times

I'd look away when you wanted most
to meet my glance? What if we knew
the instructions—*Kick your feet*

as though you were swimming and pull yourself up
—could be useful when we were breaking up?
Or later, when we tried to reunite

how we should have listened—
Once on the icy surface, stay flat,
roll away from the hole.

GHOSTS

My husband asks for a poem.
I have many, but none

to share. I live in a house
of irises where I am a ghost

searching for words
in my family's mouths.

They ask me to stop
looking and learn to cook,

love them. My husband
hands me my ring and asks why

I forget to wear it.
We smile for the photograph

only because we want to be remembered
as happy. And we are

children wanting to please
the person behind the camera

and future generations
who will see us.

I try to carry my family
in letters, in my suit pocket

as I walk to the podium
to read my poems.

They are small
ghosts in the paper.

Their meal is ginger ale
and burnt toast.

Every window in my mind
faces them, and when I turn

away, they still wave to me,
ask for their voices back.

HELPING MY PARENTS SHOP
FOR HIS & HER COFFINS

Mom touches a casket and yawns.
Death is a long overdue nap.

She likes the pale satin,
not the minty-green box.

She wants a home in the afterlife
that is worm-resistant
and a contraption to signal
the world if she is buried alive.

My dad tries to tell her this never happens,
but she says she once heard a story
about a grave they opened in Kent
and inside the coffin they found
scratch marks in the fabric of the lid.

She wants to be buried with a cellphone
or a string attached to a bell
placed above the ground.

My dad says people will bother the bell
and the silver could attract crows.

She says she's tired and these coffins
remind her of Vegas
where everything is too shiny.

My parents leave with the pamphlet
for the classic pine box.

Driving home, they talk about the sky,
how it seems to roll on forever
without a hint of fog.

HOW TO DISAPPEAR

She spent the days of December reading
Shakespeare's sonnets. Sleepy icicles dripped

from her eyelashes, but she kept reading.
Her family decorated the tree

while she sat in the leather chair reading,
opening Vendler's book when ideas failed.

She wore a discolored sweatshirt that read,
Shakespeare's Muse, carried a Mont Blanc pen

behind her ear. You could see her reading
in midnight mass near the back of the church.

While the believers knelt and prayed, she read
and worried about forgetting to shop.

The city was Christmas ghosts, lights of red.
She was buried in the snow of sonnets.

I TRY TO PLAGIARIZE MOONLIGHT

If you could sign your name to the moonlight,
that is the thing!
      —Mark Tobey

Sometimes waves scribble their initials

    over a path of moonlight. This is the closest

        to a signature I've ever seen. Maybe,

        or maybe it's the clouds with their C-curves

    crossing in front of the O—mouth open,

head thrown back and singing.

I cannot steal words if they're kept

    unspoken, but who wants to live that quietly?

        Instead, I want to swim in the dark

        sea across paper, climb the barges

    and docks that float there. Moonlight invites itself

to my desk and I try to nail its beam

to my paper. I've been swimming here

    for years, trying to steal what hasn't been

        written, diving to the bottom of an unread sea.

IF I EVER MISTAKE YOU FOR A POEM

No body was ever composed
from words, not the hipsway

of verse, the iambic beat of a heart.
Yet inside you, a sestina

of arteries, the villanelle of villi,
sonnets between your shoulder blades.

If I were more obsessive I'd follow
the alliteration of age spots across

your arms. But I have exchanged
my microscope for a stethoscope

as I want to listen inside you, past
your repetition, your free verse of skin.

How easy it is to fall for your internal
organs. Your arrhythmia is charming

hidden in the ballad of body,
your gurgling stanzas, your lyric sigh.

IN THE 70s, I CONFUSED *MACRAMÉ* AND *MACABRE*

I.

I wanted the macabre plant holder
hanging in Janet and Chrissy's apartment.
My friend said her cousin tried to kill himself
by putting his head through the patterns
in his mother's spiderplant hanger, but
the hook broke from the ceiling and he fell
knocking over their lava lamp, their 8-track player.
His brother almost died a week later when
he became tangled in the milfoil at Echo Lake.
I said, *It could have been a very*
macramé summer for that family.

II.

When I looked outside for sticks to make a God's Eye
to hang on my bedroom wall, I found a mouse
flattened, its white spine stretching past its tail.
And a few feet from that,
a dead bird with an open chest,
its veins wrapped tightly together.
This neighborhood with its macramé details
crushed into the street. I wanted
my mother to remind me
that sometimes we survive.
But when I returned to my house
it was empty, except for the macabre owl
my mother had almost finished, its body left
on the kitchen table while she ran out to buy more beads.

JOURNAL NOTES FROM A CONSULTATION
WITH A DREAM PSYCHIC

Expect a sort of heaven to appear
in your living room by Friday.

This may mean you will die soon
or that life will be easy for a while.

It depends on the angels.

Bleeding and begging angels are never a good sign.
If they were singing gospel and wearing halos,
then expect answers to circle you.

But if you wore their wings, be cautious
of bulldozers, unicycles, anything with wheels.

Yes, even cars. Good question.

Don't borrow from visitors this week.

Try to talk to the angels when they appear,
especially the one with a machete.
He has your secret. Be lucid. Soar with him.

You don't need his wings to fly. Trust me
on this. You're not the first to dream
of angels with weapons. I've known presidents
with that same type of guilt.

No, not every dream has to do with sex,
only the good ones.

And that white picket fence you observed,
it signifies peace of mind. You'll soon be free
from anxiety. Unless it was in ruins.

You may now offer my soul fifty dollars.

Your lucky number is eight.
Your power color is white.
Your psychic insect is the mirror beetle.

KYOTO

Once on the sofa
you told me, you longed
for the sofa.

And I thought you were referring
to haiku,
but you were just tired.

You don't think about art
anymore.

What you want is an organized
resumé, cherry blossoms
that don't litter the driveway.

The day I found my Yoshino cherry tree
in pieces,

I realized perfection couldn't compete
with a chainsaw.

My nostalgia carried to the truck
branch by branch.

I said nothing as nothing
was left of the tree.

You said it was scratching the van.
You said, *Dismantle.*

My bumbling arborist. My broken city.

What I wanted to say was,
You cannot restrain what is wild.

What I wanted to say was,
Collaborate.

Across the field, the cuckoo's cry
could almost be heard.

You write in your letter
something which I sometimes feel also:
Sometimes I do not know
how I shall pull through.

—Vincent van Gogh

LETTER FROM THE EMILY DICKINSON ROOM

—Sylvia Beach Hotel, Nye Beach, Oregon

I wonder what Emily would think of the view—

the ocean stretches for miles
        without houses or street signs,
the lighthouse signals to me:

        Follow through this. Follow this through.

I wonder what Emily would think
        if she knew what I really want
                is to bathe uninterrupted

with the door open,
        a candle burning near the window.

What I really want is ginger,
        bubbles, the static of sea
        whispering: *Yes. Yes, yes.*

It seems sacred
        —a woman alone in a beach town,
drying off and finding her camisole
then slipping into it, slipping off into bed.

Or maybe it's not.

Maybe it's what every woman would do
        if there were time or a place of her own
                where flickering didn't mean
there was a fire to tend, a lightbulb to replace.

When I undress again, toss my camisole
        to the floor, I think of her, Emily,
        and how she managed alone.

How we wonder about her, Emily
        the recluse, the loner,
                when we should smile
believing how thankful she was

to be with pen and paper
        listening to the wind through the oak trees,
        undressing without the help of another

and blessed to be the body between the clean sheets,
        the woman who dimmed the light.

LETTER TO A COMPANION STAR

*Astronomers looked 8,000 light-years into the cosmos with the Hubble Space Telescope,
and it seemed that the eye of God was staring back.*
                    —Editors from *National Geographic* on the Hourglass Nebula

When the doctor said,
We're only delaying death,

I forgot words and let nebulae
answer. I wrote letters
to the hospital, but did not ask,

It's all make believe, isn't it?
Instead, I saw my father
as a constellation.

When the doctor said,
He needs a miracle,

I thought my Big Bang theory
(how the world came in a Cracker Jack box)
could use some direct evidence—

funnel and horseshoe, shoe-boot
and ice skate, the old metal prizes
released from heaven.

Nebula. Nebula. Death tremor.

When I was a child, my father pointed
to sky, said, Our glass overflows with stars.

There isn't anything more we can do.

What's not half-full, but fully shattered?
Maybe I should have believed
someone was looking back

between two halos of an hourglass.
Letters went unanswered—

Aren't we always delaying death?

I did not ask.
A dying sun. A smaller star
hidden in the glow of another.

LETTER TO A PAST LIFE

When I was younger, my father said,
The broken ones become artists.

He cut the pumpkin pie
and the crust crumbled to the side.

Inside my fractured parts rattled.

Someone dropped a tray of glasses in the kitchen
and I heard them shatter.

A mother ran past holding her barefoot daughter.
A mother ran past with a broom.

A painting fell from the wall and I thought, *Listen.*

There were children hiding under tables of appetizers.
There were children painting hearts with squeeze cheese.

No one noticed my aunt, quiet with an Etch A Sketch.

I heard a mother pouring the broken glass into the garbage.
I heard her daughter say, *Snowflakes.*
I heard her daughter say, *Flakes.*

The broken ones grow up to be broken, I thought he said.
Don't worry, we can replace them. They are easy to replace.

My father asked if I wanted whipped cream or Cool Whip.
There were clouds everywhere,
all breaking apart.

LETTER TO AN ABSENTEE LANDLORD

I write letters to God
      and answers don't appear
      in words, but in blue jays

and beetles, in hummingbird
      beaks. I'm spinning
      my wings and hungry.

What God doesn't say is,
      You are not your salary.
      Practice this a million times.

God says through the honeysuckle:
      Allergy season is three weeks away.
      And sometimes: *Your father died*

and you still feel that pain. No one
      wanted my father's birdhouses.
      No one wanted years

of soap on a rope. I donated it all
      to charities. I didn't eat
      for weeks after losing

my opening act, the comedian
      with wide ties and broken body.
      Now in my reflection, veins appear,

lines where there were no lines
      before. I finger a prayer
      on a steamy bathroom mirror.

Practice this a million times.
  I dust, fill a closet with linens,
  a comforter, pillows.

What I really need is sleep,
  what I really need is the squawk
  of a blue jay to wake me up.

LETTER TO MY SISTER,
WHO IS STILL DROWNING

You tell me about the ovenbird,
its orange crown traveling swamps after sunset.

You tell me it keeps an infant under its wing
and that birds sense children underwater.

The dishes have soaked overnight
and though you know it's just your reflection
between suds, you mention Jude,
how saints appear in the waves of every body
of water.

We never talk about the summer you disappeared
into the lake, a kingfisher hovering over the shadow
of where you just were.

How I watched from land, watched water
exit from your chest, your mouth
in a burst as our father tossed you to shore
shouting:
    Breathe, breathe!

Sometimes, I don't know how to respond
when you open the refrigerator door and laugh
because you see a vision in the cantaloupe.

Someone has carved Mary into the orange center,
you say as if this world has not flooded around us,
as if everything in this life made sense.

LETTER TO VINCENT VAN GOGH,
WHO LOVED SILENCE

By the end of summer,
even moths disturbed you, their flutter
of wings against your shutters,

> a moment of paper-winged applause.
> And the tip of your pen scribbled
> too loudly against the note to your brother,

the fine hush of letters, an alphabet
of storms beneath your fingers.
And when would it end?

> Your feet scuffed the squeaky floor,
> saliva snapping in your mouth as you
> swallowed. Even your shirt scratched

as it rubbed against skin, the rush of a paintbrush
over canvas. Is that what you wanted
—the silence of bones, a deeply dug grave?

> I wonder if when you found the knife, you found
> your own way to keep the quiet of ashes, found a way
> to lower the volume of moon hanging dead in the sky.

LETTER TO WALT WHITMAN,
WHO PAINTED BUTTERFLIES

*In 1942, Whitman's handmade cardboard butterfly disappeared from the Library of Congress.
It was found in a New York attic in 1995.*

Perhaps, you made them as a child—
cardboard butterflies lining your shelves,
hiding in the pockets of the wool pants
you wore only to church.

Maybe you would wake early
to cut cardboard into small waves
forming wings, antennae appearing
like exclamation points.

Words fluttered from your pen,
cardboard wings dipped in red paint,
holding patterns of words,
the quiet swirl of wind.

Maybe there are thousands
of your butterflies still lingering in attics,
your secret world of paper insects
still hanging by threads.

MEMO TO A BUSY WORLD

When God knew the gifts He had given me
He said, *No givebacks.*

And so with flora and fauna came the spiders,
my father's disease eating through his veins.

And when I knew sadness,
God added slot machines, persimmon martinis, tabloids
of movie stars without their makeup.

He told me to wait in the longest lines.
I browsed horoscopes, bought Altoids and Star magazine.

I forgot the sweet breath of my husband sleeping
next to me. I forgot how little I arrived with.

Sometimes I notice the sunrise and I am thankful
for the sunrise.

But mostly, I return to the white face
of the monitor, the crinkled newspaper, the buzz of money.

When He whispers, I don't always hear until a city disappears
underwater, a building falls, a war begins.

He knows what He has given me
          —the blackberry bush of red-winged blackbirds,
     the song of the circling bees.

And I forget them, trying to believe I can live
on my own without being stung.

NATURAL HISTORY LESSON
ON A HIKE TO GOD'S POINT

It's not summer, but autumn
running its bony fingers up my legs.

And the leaves falling on my hair?

      A blessed-be crown for the pagan goddess
      I didn't want to become.

Today, I would much rather be indoors
shopping Saks for a long wool dress,
Donna Karan tights in forest green,

but nature has played its spirituality card
so I slip beneath a maple tree
and try to believe my life has meaning.

Sparrows sing while I consider shades
of blush: *Red in Doubt, Raisin Hell,*
Anxiety in Champagne Pink.

Sometimes I want not just contentment,
but the blue box
of sky it arrives in. Heaven City
nail polish, diamond rosary wrapped

around my cellphone—I'm connected
without sacrifice, I view the field
without touching my feet
in the dew-filled wildflowers below.

But where is my life?

> I wander through it in new leather boots,
> crushing the ladyslippers in my path.

When I come to a bear munching
on blackberries to fatten up for winter, I pause.

We see each other
like two shoppers at the same sale rack,
each rummaging through, trying to find
what we think we need to fill us up.

OTHER WORDS

We stare at the pockmarked sky,
whisper asbestos instead of clouds.

When the plane touches down
we thank Buddy Holly,
not God, Allah, or Goodness.

We say dishrag or ribtaker
instead of homemaker.
Use whiplash and lackluster
instead of breadwinner.

We say numbskull when we mean numbskull,
and blonde when we mean smart; we know
brunette is synonymous with attentive.

Let's have foxtrot instead of foreplay
and vampire bites instead of menstrual cramps.

Still, what can we substitute for childbirth?
Bamboozle? Inferno? Divinity?

There are days when sippy cups
become purgatory and family vacation
suggests space mission.

We try to talk while doing the bills,
but it turns into a mudslide. We try to speak

truthfully, but it becomes a storm watch,
tsunami warning, the dune on the beach
covered with glass.

I don't want to say fishhook
when I mean marriage, or not-tonight
when what I want to say is: I can't explain
my sadness or the night has stolen the sky.

PRAYING TO THE PATRON SAINT
OF SAVED MARRIAGES

She tells him what she cannot name—

how anger tastes as it leaves her lips,
how easy it is to love someone
            when he is sleeping,
the sound of rain as it pools
            beneath their bedroom window.

There are not enough words for sadness.

Misery and sorrow wait
            like the dead in the closets.
Melancholy loiters in the kitchen.
But how does she explain heartache
            to someone who has never
            washed night from his hair?

She unfolds the words from their corners—
comfort and *ease* tucked under their mattress,
security and *compassion* piled high
            on the bed.

She remembers how quiet their pillows were,
two faces in darkness waiting
            for the other to speak.

PREPARING LUCKY PEA SOUP IN THE NEW YEAR

She dices the peppers. Forty
degrees and falling. Last night,
her birthday and the woman she was

raised her pen to the moon,
crossed out another year, wrote *loss.*

She sees her body in the curve
of letters and not the words.

She sees the letters
she never wrote in the chili powder.

She places bacon in the skillet
and the pop of grease
surprises her, a celebration of heat.

She cannot tell you why she cried
in the spice aisle of the grocery store,

why she turned away
when she saw a friend she knew.

It's easier to suffer alone,
with a cold night and diced tomatoes.

It's easier to suffer when the moon
is your best lighting, when fine lines
appear near an open window.

She cannot imagine her life
without black-eyed peas, without

someone to share them.
She knows her husband

will return soon. She knows
she cannot push away what's already lost.

She adds a dash of cumin
because it keeps the chickens
and lovers from straying.

All of this, she stirs.

QUESTIONS AT HEAVEN'S GATE

I.

When my father meets God
he says, *Let me introduce myself. . .*

When my father meets God
he says, *Am I too early? Too late?*

When my father meets God
he says, *Do you serve drinks here?*

When my father meets God
he says, *It was easier not to believe.*

When my father meets God
he says, *I can see my house from up here.*

When my father meets God
there is only the sound of my father
falling.

When my father meets God
he says, *I can breathe again.*

When my father meets God
rain returns to the city.

II.
When God meets my father
He says, *Let me introduce myself...*

When God meets my father
He says, *Right on time, right on time.*

When God meets my father
He says, *Could I offer you an Irish Car Wreck?*

When God meets my father
He says, *It gets easier now that you're here.*

When God meets my father
He says, *I can see your house from up here.*

When God meets my father
there is only the sound of God
catching him.

When God meets my father
He says, *Welcome to your lungs.*

When God meets my father
the city is cleaned for a new life.

QUIET COLLAPSE IN THE DHARMA SHOP

I celebrate small things
    —apples, beetles, faith—
        while inside my mind

there's rattling, a broken stove
    of worry, a garden
        of hissing snakes.

I can't recognize the flowers.
    The plants are without names
        (though their poisons still sedate).

I left the garden during meditation—mosquitoes,
    craneflies. But enlightenment?
        Nowhere near my space.

Buddha. God. Universe.
    I charged spirituality
        on my VISA

—a statue of Kuan Yin, prayer flags
    to hang across the gate. But what
        might improve my mood is

a new bra and some bravery.
    Instead, I try on superstition, wear
        a D-cup of doomed fate.

I mix religions—say *chaos* and *calm*,
    corset, cheesecake—a smorgasbord
        on my plate. I am the chainsaw

carving the toothpick. A lowercase sos.
   Yesterday, I bought a silver cross.
     Magic. Amulet. Saints.

I pray to anything these days—
   the plants without names, the beetles,
     my garden of hissing snakes.

Let us go in; the fog is rising.

—Emily Dickinson

ROOFTOP MEDITATIONS

I believe I could kneel
in so many quiet places
                    —Nancy Pagh, "I Believe I Could Kneel"

Years ago
          or yesterday, I ran into the holy forest

or into Oprah's studio audience
in hope of finding peace
          or keys to a new car.

What I found was an alphabet,
a painting that read:
                    dead man.

There was a letter I wrote that said:
Sometimes I feel so disconnected.

A message from a friend:
Relax.

How I had hoped for a new car,
a life with good mileage.

Years ago
          or last night, I started a load of wash
and forgot faith

could bleed into my white sweater
or maybe it was the red towel

mixed in with everything
I love—cashmere, khakis, God,

Her white Marilyn Monroe dress
blowing over Her head
from an earthly draft below.

This is my dilemma, I said to a friend,
How can I know God if there's no God?

She said faith sticks to the roof
of my house, has its own ringtone.

Years ago
        or this morning I was scraping moss
off the roof and meditating
on these words

—*call me, calm me*—

I was waiting for the hospital bill,
for the car accident to happen,
for a thousand things to go wrong.

This was when the phone rang,
when I heard church bells
through the fogbank,

sometimes I feel so disconnected

my caller ID blinking
Unknown * Unknown.

How many years have I waited
for my A-ha! moment?

Hello? I said
to my imagined tragedies,
then a click

and there was nothing—

how quiet God was
when She finally phoned.

SAID PRAYER

I begin with the facts—the word Sunday
is not in the Bible.
Neither is daisy, hibiscus.

I whisper apple peels, braided vine,
passion fruit, kiwi.

The fruit fly was the first insect in space.

I pray and hear myself speaking
to ghosts. Old prayer.

I return to what I know—
2,036 nuclear bomb explosions
since World War II.

The word hummingbird
is not in the Bible.

Sometimes it's okay to be terrified.
House spider, bumblebee.

In the shower with water
and cupped hands, I breathe in
steam, draw a rocket on foggy glass.

I pray in safety razors and blood. Honey
and 90% of plane crashes have survivors.

I speak stamens of afternoon
gardens, earthworms and their five
hearts. *Keep my family safe.*

Once I saw Mary on a mushroom
cloud. Old keychain. Atoms for peace.
On the other side—a saint.

Even on the clearest days,
I can't recognize the honeysuckle from
the red plastic feeder. Still, I sip and gather.

SELECTED LOVE LETTERS
I'M STILL TRYING TO WRITE

When Dylan wrote to Cat, he misspelled
Indiana and I misspell when I'm in love,

misspell *men* for *me*, misspell *room*
for *roam*. My letters tell another story,
they cry of a slow hang
and not a slow hand.

When I translate sex as a string of firecrackers,
there is always one position I can't pronounce.

Sometimes I dot my *i*'s with mascara.
Sometimes I don't see myself as *y*'s.

I am the handwriting of a car crash,
bent metal and adrenalin-filled.
I walk away from the accident,
say:

> *We could have been.*

A buzzard circles the freeway
and his call is similar to a cat's.
The bird writes love letters to the injured
driver in the other car.

When I insist on walking home,
the letters I write are my footprints,
the fig leaves I tear from the tree.

There's an empty envelope
outside my home, a broken pen
on the doorstep.
         I'm not in love
with the mail carrier,
I'm in love with what he holds.

Once I wrote a letter to a lover
in black widow bites: *My bug,
sometimes venom is only words.*

SONG OF THE SORRY LOVERS

Ted Hughes was resting on his side,
bottom shelf and dusty.
Birthday Letters, now $5.50,
slightly more than the caramel Frappuccino
I purchased just to use the Starbucks' bathroom.
The barista with the mermaid tattoo
on his forearm handed me the key
attached to a giant spoon and said,
There's room in there for two, if you're lonely.

Ted Hughes was saying, *You want this,*
but what I wanted was the half-Cuban firefighter
whose license plate read *Fuego.*
Earlier, I visited the station
hoping for a glance, but he was asleep
in his bunk room, deep in the back
and didn't hear me when I dropped my purse.
I imagined him, undusty,
on his side dreaming of women
he's not married to.

Ted Hughes was begging, sale price,
*You've avoided me so far, but I've felt you finger
my pages.* I tried to tell him
about my relationship with his first wife,
how I met her in high school,
even named my cat Sylvia.
If I brought him home,
they'd have to share a shelf
and if I pulled out Sexton, they'd touch.
Still, I could hear him whispering as I left,
Take me. You know you want to.

SPEECH LESSONS

The fewer words the better prayer.
               —Martin Luther

Because the girl didn't speak
until she was sixteen,
when she spoke

a bicycle rolled from her tongue,
spinning down a hill

past the stop sign, a red sink
of pots to the dyslexic housewife,

past a charm of goldfinches,
a storytelling of ravens,
an alphabet of jays,

past a mailbox of chain letters
and the mailman humming
a bag filled with notes.

Because the girl confused language
for languor, she rested her head
on a pillow and the bicycle

crashed into the headboard,
wheels spinning, spokes
flying into prayer.

THEORIES OF A GARDEN ASTRONOMER

If one could conclude as to the nature of the Creator from a study of this creation it would appear that God has a special fondness for stars and beetles.
            —J.B.S. Haldane, British geneticist 1892-1964

Because I offered iris to the earth,
buried bulbs deep beneath soil,
I saw the mirror beetle appear in the garden.

I opened my hand and the beetle
flew to my palm, a miracle
beneath wing-coverings.

I passed the bamboo and noticed the universe
in a web, a red spider nebula,
a Beehive Cluster circling above.

Later when I looked to Scarabaeus,
the beetle made from stars, I wondered
if it was easier to trust a constellation.

Insects vanished, came and went
with the seasons, but stars circled
a dependable dance on the ceiling.

I planted more bulbs and the beetle appeared
again. Slowly I'm learning how life's created
from a galaxy of surprise occasions

—wind chimes playing a concerto
for moths, a damselfly sewing the last stitch
of summer to August's fallen hem.

The mirror beetle arrived daily.
As I held the insect, the cocoon I wore
began to unravel while Betelgeuse brightened

Orion's shoulder. And here on earth,
I trusted chance a little more
and the glow mirrored in my hand.

UNDER THE COVERS WE FIND JESUS

Under the covers we find a picture of Jesus
and you say your mother was cleaning
the guest room,
          cleaning and it must have fallen
from the wall.

          You say your mother, a neatnik,
was cleaning and she didn't leave Jesus
in our bed as a reminder,
          the reminder we're not married.

It's not a sign of our soon-to-be sin,
Jesus in our bed, an accident, a misplaced Lord.

There is a small plastic Mary on the dresser.
          You say, *If she wanted to scare us,*
Mary would be upside down on the pillow.

Still, Jesus appeared in his thorny crown as I pulled
down the sheets, Jesus and his soft brown eyes,
so welcoming,   so forgiving,

Jesus, sweet Jesus

with lips like yours, pink and ready to kiss
goodbye to this evening, this faithful evening

of figs left on the counter
by your mother, figs and a loaf of fresh bread
she baked with faithful hands.

UNIVERSE VIEWING FROM HOME

I've canceled the blue moon
and the lunar eclipse.

I'm requesting cash back
for the night I spent in a parking lot,
binoculars in hand searching for Hale-Bopp.

There is no reason to revisit the sky
so many times in a life.

Think bed slippers, ceiling fan.

Let's not set our alarms for three a.m.,
the best viewing time for the Orionid meteor shower.

Instead, watch me flick embers
across our living room,
say sevenish?

I'll point as it passes: *Did you see it?*
You can say, *No.*
The miracle recreated.

Let's not put our faith in astronomers,
they are still discovering moons for Jupiter.
Four years ago, eleven more.

Where were they hiding?

Let's not put our faith in anyone
until they begin naming moons after poets.

Neruda is a minor planet, number 1875.
Neruda has a crater-in-waiting on Mercury.

Give me a poem, a book, a body to revolve around
in our cluttered cosmos.

Let me climb beneath this blue night,
blue moon, blue comforter pulled far above our heads.

THE VANISHING POEMS OF EMILY DICKINSON

Emily Dickinson got so drunk on dew that she was reeling around and the angels were hanging over the edge of heaven and waving their snowy hats. It's one of her lesser known poems.
—Nelson Bentley

I know this poem.

This is the one where the sky is a swim-up bar
and they're serving rainwater mixed with ice cubes of hail.

Isn't this the poem
where we lose ourselves in her clothes?
        No, someone's undressing her.

Or maybe it's an early draft,
        Emily not only drinks dew, but falls
                into a rabbit hole, sings her poems
to the tune of *Camptown Races*—

I'm nobody. Who are you? Who are you? Who are you?

Okay, I need some help here—Emily's drunk
        and angels lean carelessly.   Ah, college!
                I remember last call and touching men
with blonde wings, while women in white boas
        dropped feathers from balconies.

And I've lived this poem,
except one Saturday when I stayed home in bed
reading poetry.

That evening every word
        was my drink, Vodka Collins drowning
        both angels and hats.

The edge of heaven—
        I can't believe there is such a place

where I look up or down depending
on whether I'm visiting Emily
or just holding her
        in my lap, her small head
            resting against my knees.

WHAT THE UNIVERSE MAKES OF LINGERIE

It's impossible to see a black bra
directly as no light can escape from it,
still there are supernovas, dark matter,

meteorites in its path. The black bra
understands its usefulness is overrated.
It's problematic under a white

shirt of a white woman, unprofessional
peeking out of a blazer. To see
observational evidence of black bras

you do not need to borrow
the Hubble Telescope to view the Hourglass
Nebula, their existence is well-supported,

a gravitational field so strong
nothing can escape. Black bras
can be found in the back of a Vega

between the vinyl seats. It is the star
the boy wishes on—he is never the master
of the unhook, Orion unfastening

his constellation belt. Let it remain
a mystery, something almost seen,
almost touched in a Galaxy. I'd call it

rocketworthy, but there is cosmic
censorship, naked singularities
to consider. The black bra has electric

charge, too close to the event horizon,
a man disappears in its loophole, escape
velocity equal to the speed of light.

XANAX PRESCRIPTION GOES UNFILLED

—explaining to my doctor why I don't want medication

I know you view me as an *anxious person,*
        a *sour expansion* of what's considered
        normal,

but if you give me *medication,*
        I fear it could be my creative *decimation.*

Let me *trust my emotions*
        because even in *my nuttiest rooms,*

I find *safety in words.* I *satisfy wonder,*
to *alphabetize* is to *baptize* and *heal.*

All through my day, I find happiness
        in *revising poems, imposing verse*

on a world that reads *gossip columns* while the *pulsing cosmos*
spins towards every *black hole,* every *bleak loch.*

Yes, when I'm off course, *any exit* leads to *anxiety*—

watch me *traveling the road* with *heartland vertigo,*
but I don't need to be *less manic*—
        Miss Clean
        I, Calmness.

So before you *offer medication* to create *a fiction freedom,*
allow me to move *towards poetry* to *postdate worry.*

No, Dr. Xanax, Dr. Looking-for-your-little-pad,

Let me get though this
without you.
Let me

echo poems

as with that
as with that

comes hope.

YAKIMA FERRY AT SUNSET

Tonight I could write a thousand poems
no one should have to read.

All around me are hippie grandmothers
and grey-haired men with dreamcatchers

hanging from the rearview mirrors of their
Hondas. Everyone is irresistible tonight:

the man in his NRA t-shirt, the child
on the upper deck screaming about licorice,

the woman who cut in front of me to buy a latte.
I am skimming the edges like every poet

on this boat, starting my sentences
with the easiest words—*I love, I love, I love*

to travel home by ferry, the women
who smile at the men they don't know,

how my tongue feels in my mouth,
a sort of heaviness that never leaves.

YEAR OF THE METEOR SHOWER

I see fireflies instead of stars, stars
     instead of meteors.

I suggest that as much as I adore the moon,
     maybe it's too bright.

You tell me the moon is slowly moving away
     from earth and I'll have my darkness

soon enough. It's been sixteen years
     since we watched the moon rise

in Mexico, watched the waitress reach for my hand
     and say my wedding band was a sky

layered in stars. I told her it's easy to be fooled
     by diamonds, by falling stars.

On the flight home, I was reading a romance
     novel when lightning struck the plane.

Meteors and honeymooners sparked
     over a country and the plane continued on.

When I leaned in and said, *I'm afraid*
     to die, you told me the whole world

has this secret. Behind us, two women
     began praying, asked saints to keep the plane

in the air. We were not born with wings
     like fireflies, we've had to invent what holds us

up. I reached for your hand hoping to land
        safely in Seattle and the thought of losing

what we had found together flickered,
        or maybe, an overhead bulb

needed to be replaced. Outside my window,
        skyscrapers brightened our descent

as we headed towards the runway
        in a country layered with light.

You whispered (and I could almost see
        the glimmer inside you),

Too much city, not enough stars.

YEARS LATER, A FULL SPICE RACK

for Rosendo

You make me vegetable curry
and I am too hungry to taste it.

You love my garden.
I plant a fence.

There are lentils on your shirt.
The untouched roasted garlic

is the moon. The moon is
the unnoticed Gaelic prayer

I whisper when you are sleeping.
Let me be your absentminded

lover, the split wishbone
confusing broke for misery. I sing

in your dreams—*Ár n-arán laethuil
tabhair duinn inniu*—

and when your hands open,
I look from your emptiness,

everything and too much, half
a fig and you give me more.

I sew poverty to my blouse
and blame you for providing

the thread and needle. You stitch me
a new shirt with pockets full

of cinnamon. I open my lips and your breath
fills me. Tonight it is enough.

ZEN AND THE ART OF LEAVING

If you awake after I've gone—

I cleaned the glass on the woodstove
   with wet newspaper.

I didn't mean to use the comics or the front page,
   but you didn't miss much—

the headlines were the same, and Sally hit Linus
   with her lunchbox

because he threw away her valentine.
   A salmon laid eggs in the river

this morning (another type of valentine).
   She turned sideways, glistened silver.

If the large white rock was Nevada,
   she was Seattle. Yesterday, she was Oregon.

I am still searching for my book
   about beetles. If you find it, mail it to me.

I'm pressing iris beneath the front cover.
   On the table, a hat I found. Yours?

I have thrown away the stale crumb cake
   and bitter tea. You might see my worries

in the water; I left them to float downstream
   into the world of what didn't happen,

into the sea of what went right.
      There were deer tracks near the river

where the elk bones rest—life and death
      —both beautiful and unexpected.

Visit them before the rain erases the red soil.
      I have shut the door, but did not lock it.

ZINA'S HOOKAH LOUNGE

I wonder if I've been changed in the night?
　　　　　　—Alice from *Alice in Wonderland* by Lewis Carroll

In the corner booth, a belly dancer
eats baklava while old men play cards.
Smoke drifts through the room.

We sample dolmas, baba ghanoush
at a table that wobbles
when we lift our chai.

Hummus mingles with tabouli.
Parsley escapes from the plate.
The men next to us smoke, keep smoking

as a woman stops to ask them,
What's inside your bong?
When a man answers, *Pleasure,*

she sits down, puts on her lipstick
in the reflection on the hookah.

It's last call and you buy us passion
fruit martinis, say,
Before we go, let's try a drink.

Smoke circles and a hazy calligraphy
fills us like the caterpillar
atop the mushroom—*who are you?*

Some nights we aren't sure
what brings us comfort,
but we take it all in—

belly dancer, baklava, chai.
We are not rich, but full
of spices, honey cake, and tea.

NOTES ON THE POEMS:

"Another Empty Window Dipped in Milk": The title of this poem was taken from a line in Carolyn Forche's poem, "On Earth" from *Blue Hour*. "Spiritus mundi" translates to "spirit of the world," reflecting the idea that we are all connected. The actual quote by Albert Einstein is, "There are two ways to live: you can live as if nothing is a miracle; you can live as if everything is a miracle."

"Being Called Back": The line *dressed as a broom* is from Pablo Neruda's poem, "Nothing But Death."

"Believing Anagrams," "Fragments of a Dissected Word," and "Xanax Prescription Goes Unfilled": Each poem uses anagrams throughout it. The anagrammed words are italicized, so they are more easily recognized.

"Coming Up Next: How Killer Blue Irises Spread": The correct title of the misheard NPR report was "How Killer Flu Viruses Spread."

"Preparing Lucky Pea Soup in the New Year":
The full recipe for LUCKY PEA SOUP is—

INGREDIENTS
- · 4 slices bacon
- · I green bell pepper, chopped
- · I small onion, chopped
- · 2 (15 ounce) cans black-eyed peas, undrained
- · 2 (14.5 ounce) cans diced tomatoes, undrained
- · I cup water
- · I 1/2 teaspoons salt
- · I 1/4 teaspoons cumin
- · I 1/4 teaspoons dry mustard
- · I teaspoon chili powder
- · 1/2 teaspoon curry powder
- · 1/2 teaspoon pepper
- · 1/2 teaspoon sugar

DIRECTIONS

Place the bacon in a skillet and cook over medium-high heat until crisp and evenly brown. Drain on paper towels. When cool, crumble into small pieces. Using the same skillet, add the peppers and onion; stir and cook over medium-high heat until transparent and tender, about 5 minutes. Pour the black beans, tomatoes, and water into a large pot. Stir in the peppers, onion, salt, cumin, dry mustard, chili powder, curry powder, pepper, and sugar. Bring to a boil, reduce heat to medium, cover, and simmer 20 to 25 minutes. Make a wish. Serve hot sprinkled with bacon and other toppings of your choice.

"Rooftop Mediations": This poem is dedicated to Nancy Pagh and was inspired by her poem, "I Believe I Could Kneel" from her book, *No Sweeter Fat*.

"Song of the Sorry Lovers": The title of this poem was taken from a poem by Ted Hughes published in *Chequer* in 1954 and the half-Cuban firefighter now works as a mail carrier in Florida.

"Theories of a Garden Astronomer": The Mirror Beetle is an enchanted insect created by glass artist Roger Nachman. The beetle has the scientific name: *Elypticum Reflectiva*.

"Years Later, A Full Spice Rack": *Ár n-arán laethuil tabhair duinn inniu* is Irish Gaelic for "Give us this day our daily bread" from "The Lord's Prayer."

Kelli Russell Agodon was born and raised in Seattle and educated at the University of Washington and Pacific Lutheran University's Rainier Writers Workshop where she received her MFA in creative writing. She is the author of *Small Knots* (2004) and *Geography*, winner of the 2003 Floating Bridge Press Chapbook Award.

Her work has appeared in literary magazines and anthologies such as the *Atlantic Monthly, Prairie Schooner, Notre Dame Review, North American Review, Image, 5 a.m, Meridian, Crab Orchard Review, Calyx, The Seattle Review, Poets Against the War* edited by Sam Hamill, as well as on NPR's "The Writer's Almanac" with Garrison Keillor and in Keillor's second anthology, *Good Poems for Hard Times* (Viking Press).

Kelli is a recipient of three Washington State Artist Trust GAP grants, the James Hearst Poetry Prize, the Dorothy Rosenberg Poetry Prize, the William Stafford Award, the Carlin Aden Award for formal verse, a Soapstone Writer's Residency, and a grant from the Puffin Foundation for her work towards peace and as a poetry editor for the broadside series, The Making of Peace.

Currently, Kelli lives in a seaside community in the Northwest with her family. She is the co-editor of Seattle's literary journal, *Crab Creek Review.* Visit her website at: www.agodon.com

Acknowledgments *(continued from copyright page)*

"Letter to My Sister, Who is Still Drowning": *Bellevue Literary Review*
"Letter to Vincent Van Gogh, Who Loved Silence": *Redactions*
"Letter to Walt Whitman, Who Painted Butterflies": *North American Review*
"Natural History Lesson On a Hike to God's Point": *Superstition Review*
"Other Words": *Poetry Northwest*
"Praying to the Patron Saint of Saved Marriages": *5 a.m.*
"Questions at Heaven's Gate": *Image*
"Said Prayer": *Escape into Life*
"Selected Love Letters I'm Still Trying to Write": *The Smoking Poet*
"Song of the Sorry Lovers": *Ginger Hill*
"Speech Lessons": *Coal Hill Review*
"Under the Covers We Find Jesus": *Rhino*
"Universe Viewing From Home": *Atlanta Review*
"The Vanishing Poems of Emily Dickinson": *Natural Bridge*
"What the Universe Makes of Lingerie": *Notre Dame Review*
"Yakima Ferry at Sunset": *5 a.m.*
"Year of the Meteor Shower": *Escape into Life*
"Years Later, A Full Spice Rack": *Jeanne Lohmann Award, OPN Online*
"Zen and The Art of Leaving": *North American Review*
"Zina's Hookah Lounge": *diode*

Many thanks to the faculty and participants at Pacific Lutheran University's Rainier Writers Workshop including Stan Rubin, Judith Kitchen, Sharon Bryan, Albert Goldbarth, and Peggy Shumaker—without you, many of these poems would have never been written.

Thank you to my tribe of writers for your ongoing support: Annette Spaulding-Convy, Jennifer Culkin, Nancy Canyon, Ronda Broatch, Jeannine Hall Gailey, Martha Silano, Susan Rich, Kathleen Flenniken, Holly Hughes, Jenifer Lawrence, Lana Hechtman Ayers, Nancy Pagh, Ann Batchelor Hursey, Janet Norman Knox, Natasha Moni, Michael Schmeltzer, and John Davis. Thank you for always being there for me.

Thank you Susie Cramer, Janice & Dale Cramer, Lisa Fritzer, Suzanne Hermanson, Kari Pelaez Golden, and Marcia Randall DeBard for your encouragement and friendship.

Special thanks to Artist Trust, the Dorothy Rosenberg Prize, Soapstone Writers Residency, the Puffin Foundation, all wonderful organizations who gave me time or funding for my work.

Many thanks to the Sylvia Beach Hotel in Nye Beach, Oregon where many of these poems were written. May the Emily Dickinson Room continue to inspire.

Thank you Dennis Maloney and Carl Dennis for choosing my manuscript—I am extremely grateful for your belief in my work.

And most of all, my deepest love and appreciation to my family who has supported me throughout my entire journey as a writer: Rose & Delaney, thank you with as much love as I can type. I love you both more than words. And much love and thanks to my mother, Gloria Russell-Baker, who always believed in me and taught me to be a dreamer in a wide-awake world. I owe you everything. Thank you, Mum! I love you.

The White Pine Press Poetry Prize